Orangutans
For Kids

Amazing Animal Books
For Young Readers

By
Rachel Smith

Mendon Cottage Books

JD-Biz Publishing

Amazing Animal Book Series

Download Free Books!
http://MendonCottageBooks.com

Table of Contents

Introduction 4

What is an orangutan?..5

How do orangutans act? 9

The history of orangutans and humans..18

Orangutans and culture...21

Orangutans and conservation 24

Conclusion...26

Author Bio..27

Publisher 33

Introduction

The orangutan is probably one of the more fascinating apes in existence. Less people know a lot about it compared to animals like the chimpanzee and the gorilla, but they certainly have their own charms.

A red ape with very long arms, the orangutan looks kind of silly. But it has intelligence that surpasses its appearance, and has fascinated scientists and storytellers alike for centuries.

What is an orangutan?

The orangutan is sometimes called the orangutang, the orang-utan, and so on. It is from Indonesia and Malaysia originally, two countries that are considered part of Asia.

A young orangutan

However, nowadays, you can only find it in two places: the rainforests of Borneo, and the rainforests of Sumatra. Borneo is the largest island in Asia, and is split between three countries: Brunei, Indonesia, and Malaysia. The largest part of it belongs to Indonesia. Sumatra is a smaller island that belongs entirely to Indonesia.

The orangutan is the in the genus Pongo. It is the only member of the subfamily Ponginae, which once contained other apes, such as the genus Gigantopithecus. The three members of the genus Gigantopithecus are most known for being some of the largest apes the world has ever seen; however, all we have to know they existed is mostly teeth (over a thousand) and a few jaw bones.

On the other hand, the orangutan obviously exists. We are able to see them in modern day rainforests.

The orangutan is well-known for its long reach; it has very long arms compared to its body, especially if you compare them to a human's. They have short, bowed legs, meaning that they're sort of bent. A human baby's legs tend to be somewhat bowed, but this is something they grow out of. Orangutans don't.

They are also covered in reddish-brown fur, which is a stark contrast to the black fur of most great apes. The gorilla, for instance, is almost completely black. Not so with the orangutan. It has gray-black sort of skin, often misrepresented as blue.

The males and females, at least, fully grown adults, are what are called sexually dimorphic. This simply means that females and males look different; di means two, and morphic refers to appearance. So, a male tends to have not only a throat pouch to make loud calls, but also cheek flaps. These flaps are kind of big, and only appear on fully-grown males. A young male looks just like a female.

Males are also considerably bigger, with arm spans of up to 6.6 feet. That's wider than most humans are tall. A male also can weight up twice as much as a female, or more.

Some males may also have a sort of mustache or beard thing going on.

Orangutans have different hands to humans. Their fingers are longer, and tend to naturally, when resting, curve. Their thumbs are smaller and less nimble than humans' thumbs. However, their hands are very well adapted to living in the trees; they can hang from their hands for a long time, much longer than a human could, and even without their thumb, they can pick up small objects pretty easily.

Their feet are somewhat similar to their hands, very much unlike humans. They have four long toes and then a big opposable toe. An opposable finger or toe is like the thumb on humans; it allows us to do a lot more than animals with just paws or especially things like flippers. The opposable digit makes for better grip and maneuverability, meaning that we can do more delicate and intricate tasks.

The opposable toe on the orangutan's foot allows it a lot of ability to do things with its feet. It can pick up things just about as easily with its feet as with its hands.

This makes sense when you remember where the orangutan lives: the rainforest. The rainforest is thick with trees, and the orangutan very rarely leaves the trees. So, feet that can grip are much more useful than feet like a human's, which are made for walking on the ground.

Their hips are also very flexible, so their legs can move differently and with a wider range than with humans. It's a similar story with their other joints, such as their shoulders.

The gorilla, for example, walks on its knuckles. However, the orangutan is different its great ape cousins, and instead walks on its fists.

Another thing about the orangutan is that, as an ape, it has no tail. Paraphrased, a monkey has a tail, but if it has a monkey shape and no tail, it's typically an ape.

So, note that an orangutan is an ape and not a monkey, which is an easy mistake to make.

How do orangutans act?

Orangutans are interesting creatures, though they do share a lot of behavior with other apes. However, the orangutan is still a very unique creature, and has its own world of behaviors.

A mother and her baby orangutan.

For one thing, an orangutan eats fruit. However, they will eat other things too, such as eggs, bark, honey, insects, and leaves. They're called opportunistic eaters, which means they will eat what they can, to an extent.

They are primarily fruit eaters, though. It varies a lot from month to month, but their diet can be made up of anywhere from 45 percent fruit to ninety percent fruit. They much prefer rainforests where there's a lot of sugary or fatty pulp fruit. It gives the most nutrition, after all.

The orangutan spends much of its time eating. It's a good two to three hours in the morning that is spent eating. After that, they rest for a while, and towards the evening, they make up their nests for the night. An orangutan must eat a good deal, as fruits are just not as high-calorie as some other foods, such as meat.

Orangutans are the ape that spends the most amount of time in trees. However, there is little reason to leave, as the fruits are in the trees, as is most of what they need.

They can't swim, though they have been known to wade. An orangutan can be on the ground and even in the water, but it really prefers not to be.

The main issue when it comes to predators is the tiger. Other predators include creatures such as the clouded leopard, wild dogs, and of course, the crocodile. The tiger is not the same issue on Borneo as the other habitat, because it simply doesn't live on Borneo. But the other predators apply.

In the case of wild dogs, it's an infestation that affects many places. Dogs have lived throughout much of the world for a long time, but more recently, in the past couple hundred years or so, the wild dog population has become a problem.

In places like Borneo, where dogs simply did not exist before humans brought them there, the wild dogs add an extra predator where there was no such predator before. It means more competition for food resources, and unfortunately, there are few animals that hunt wild dogs.

This is an issue throughout much of the more isolated world, such as Australia and island nations.

The orangutans from Sumatra have been known to live at higher altitudes than the Bornean ones, by a good five hundred feet or so.

They will also live in mountainous areas and swampy areas, not just your typical rainforest.

A way orangutans communicate is through sounds. One such example is the long call that the male orangutan makes. This is loud, and is used to both attract females, and let other males know they're there.

Another sound is the rolling call, which is sort of a guttural sound. Both sexes use this sound, as a sort of intimidation tactic. This means they try to scare away the other orangutan, typically by not fighting.

The orangutan, when annoyed, will suck air through sort of 'kissy lips', makng a sound folks call a kiss squeak. Baby orangutans also make soft hoots.

Orangutans tend to make raspberries too. It's funny, because most humans think only human children make raspberries, but the orangutan does too.

Orangutans are very important in their environments. It's believed that they may be the only ones who spread the seeds of some fruits.

Another interesting thing is that sometimes, they eat dirt or rocks. There are three reasons they might do this: one is to get minerals they're not getting in their diet that they need. Another is to combat diarrhea, which goes to show how smart they are. The last is to ingest clay, which can be used to absorb toxic stuff.

The orangutan is very smart. It's an intelligent creature that uses tools. One example of its intelligence is its use of a particular plant as an anti-inflammatory. Inflammation is when there's bad germs somewhere in the animal's body, and so the cells that fight bad germs build up there. It often makes the skin red and kind of puffy, depending on where it is.

Orangutans have figured out how to treat that, as well as the previously mentioned treatment for diarrhea.

They have been known to come up with large numbers of tools for getting at insects and fruit. However, this varies from group to group, showing that these skills are cultural and therefore passed on to the next generation or throughout the group.

The orangutan is also potentially good at linguistics. Linguistics is the study of language, or the field of language. While they certainly can't talk or learn to speak a human language, since their mouths and minds are not quite adapted to it, they have been shown to learn sign language.

However, this sign language is very simple, the same kind taught to gorillas. In this case, it's not a sign language deaf, hearing impaired, or mute people use, such as British Sign Language or American Sign Language (which are distinctly different languages). Instead, it's a modified sign language.

In this sign language, there aren't the same sentence structures and other things as in a normal language. This is because the ape doesn't think in sentences like humans do.

The orangutans who were taught this modified sign language were able to learn between thirty and forty signs in the sign language each, and were able to communicate using them. The same sort of techniques were applied as with Koko the gorilla, the famous gorilla who learned how to sign.

The social structure of the orangutan is different from humans. Orangutans are the most solitary of the great apes, though they are not entirely alone.

A female, typically with a baby, will have her own home range; close by will be about seven or less other females' home ranges, and they're often related to the female.

All of these ranges will be within a male's range, and he is their mate. The males will not allow their ranges to overlap much with another male's, and in fact, full grown males often fight over their ranges.

Females sometimes fight, but other times, females get along very well. For the most part, orangutans can be described as solitary but social.

For transient females and males, the rules are a little different. Transient means that they don't have a home range, and sort of wander. It's sort of the same idea behind human hoboes; they travel to find what they need, such as food, with no home to speak of.

These orangutans, both transient and ones with homes, will meet up in the same large fruit trees to eat together. Because there is so much fruit, there's very little competition, and so the orangutans are not likely to fight.

For orangutans who aren't adults, they very often do travel in small groups together. The only way for a male to get his own territory is to oust a dominant male from his range, and take over that area. This means that orangutan males who are not quite adults have to be transient for a while.

Females, on the other hand, tend to make their ranges just outside of their mother's. However, they can be transient too.

Orangutans also build nests. Nest-building is very important to orangutans, and the skill is passed on to babies pretty early. By the age of three years, a young orangutan can expertly build a nest. They have been known to add all kinds of features to their nests, all the way up to bunk beds of sorts!

What kinds of orangutans are there?

There are two kinds of orangutans, and then some subspecies.

The main two types of orangutans are the Bornean orangutan, and the Sumatran orangutan. They are considered two separate species, and probably separated about 400,000 years ago. This makes sense, because they are quite separated by the sea.

In the case of the Bornean orangutan, there are three subspecies. These three represent different groups of orangutans that live in parts of Borneo.

First, there's the northwest population. Then, there's the eastern population. Lastly, there's the southwest population.

There's really not much difference among them to the naked eye. It's mostly zoologists who care about classifying them among subspecies. The average person would not note much difference at all.

The debate about whether or not these are two different species still goes on. As with most animals, nothing is particularly clear-cut. Since there are so many similarities, it can be difficult to know for sure.

The division into two species is a very recent one. It was done in 1996, which is about twenty years ago. While that is a very long time for the average human, it's very short in scientific history. It's like your brother discovering he's actually left-handed instead of right-handed just yesterday, after many years of believing he was right-handed.

A male orangutan.

The history of orangutans and humans

The history of orangutans and humans is an interesting one. First off, of course, are the native peoples of Borneo and Sumatra.

The people who have lived there for farther back than human memory has recorded have known about orangutans for millennia. That's thousands of years.

Many groups of native peoples have stories and traditions about the orangutan. For one thing, while many groups did hunt, eat, and decorate with the orangutan, other groups absolutely would not. Some even considered it bad luck to look it in the face.

A frequent story is that of the orangutan kidnapping humans. Sometimes, they even mate with them. Another typical story has the male hunter being seduced by a female orangutan. These peoples recognized the orangutan's similarity to humans pretty easily, and many of them found it unnerving or scary.

Europeans discovered the orangutan for Western society in about the 17th century, probably. And in the 19th century, they were very extensively hunted; a lot of people wanted stuffed orangutans or other prizes to show their hunting prowess.

But very little was actually known about the orangutan. It's only been fairly recent that we've learned anything about its actual behavior and such.

We owe this knowledge to a very determined and smart woman, who is named Biruté Galdikas. She is a Canadian woman who traveled to Borneo several decades ago, and lived in a thatched hut for about thirty years.

A seated male orangutan.

She extensively studied the orangutans, one of three women selected to be supported in studying apes in their natural habitat by Dr. Louis Leakey. The others, first being Jane Goodall, who studied chimpanzees, while living amongst them, and secondly, Dian Fossey, who studied mountain gorillas, are well-known like Biruté is for opening up the world of apes.

Galdikas is the world's foremost expert on orangutans, and she works hard to advocate for them and help them. She helps orphaned orangutans, and though she has had controversy in some of her life with her work, she genuinely works for the conservation of apes.

The world also seems to be moving steadily towards granting apes that bear similarities to humans more rights. Argentina, for example, ruled in an orangutan named Sandra's favor that she should be moved to Brazil. This was to grant her freedom, as she was in a zoo, and instead was to be moved to a sanctuary, which allows a lot more space and natural habitat.

Some groups have interpreted the ruling as allowing all animals such freedom, but according to legal experts, it's only the 'hominid apes', that is, apes similar to humans, that this applies to.

This is probably because such apes are considered intelligent, and humans hate to think that something that can think is suffering. It's a moral dilemma that has more recently risen to the surface: is it justifiable to make an intelligent creature suffer? And if not, what exactly qualifies as an intelligent creature? Is it only ones who can, for example, learn modified sign language? Count numbers? Use tools?

This is a hazy grey subject, and it will probably be debated a lot in the future.

Orangutans and culture

Orangutans are a part of the Indonesian and Malaysian cultures for sure, but they have affected the world as well. They have been in zoos throughout the world, but also in the media throughout the world.

One example of a famous orangutan is Ken Allen. He was a Bornean orangutan who lived at the San Diego zoo. He was famous for escaping constantly. He was very clever, and would figure out how to do things like unscrew bolts. He was not dangerous, though, and a common end to his escapes was a visitor walking him back to a zookeeper, simply holding his hand.

A little orangutan.

An example of fictional orangutan in culture is in the book *Melincourt*. This book was written and published about 1817, so undoubtedly there are a lot of inaccuracies about how orangutans actually function.

It's a book in which an orangutan, named Sir Oran Haut-Ton is made to act like a human, and is made a candidate for the Parliament, the governing body of the United Kingdom. Of course, the idea is silly, but it related to the actual issue of the time. The idea was that the orangutan represented leaders of a certain part of the society that got their posts easily, so it was meant to mock people in power.

A rather well-known fictional orangutan is the ape King Louie in Disney's the Jungle Book. This is a movie that was fairly popular, based on the story by Rudyard Kipling, a famous children's author. The character of King Louie actually wasn't in the original story, and was instead added in by Disney.

Lastly, in the Donkey Kong series by Nintendo, there's also the character of Lanky Kong. He is seen in a few games, and considered a distant member of the Kong family.

There are quite a few more examples of orangutans in media, though most of the time they're meant to be a joke.

Orangutans and conservation

Conservation of orangutans and their habitat is a serious issue. Because of many things, including gold mining and excessive hunting, the orangutan has become endangered. The Bornean is less endangered than the Sumatran, but both are at risk.

A mother and baby orangutan.

Another thing that really has hurt the orangutan populations is the extensive logging and the forest fires. Both have taken out a lot of habitat and orangutans.

The reason so much of their habitat has been destroyed was so that palm oil plantations could be built. Palm oil is valuable, used for many things, and it requires a decent amount of space to grow a big crop. It's used for things like cooking, cosmetics, and biodiesel. The reason for the growth of such plantations was that the world wanted more, and so, people responded to that.

It doesn't make it right, but the thing to remember in countries like these is that often, it seems like the people of the country have to make a choice between earning a decent living and their natural surroundings.

It's also unfortunately common for orangutan mothers to be killed, and their babies sold as pets. These babies usually don't do well, and some of the time, they are rescued by the government.

In general, there's a lot of work to be done if the orangutan is to be saved.

Hopefully, the world is up to it.

Conclusion

The orangutan is a quirky, interesting animal. It is incredibly intelligent, and deserves the attention it gets.

Hopefully, even with all its problems, it will do well, and people will recognize that the orangutan is an animal worth working to keep. Because if we don't do something, like many other animals throughout the world, it could disappear.

Author Bio

Rachel Smith is a young author who enjoys animals. Once, she had a rabbit who was very nervous, and chewed through her leash and tried to escape. She's also had several pet mice, who were the funniest little animals to watch. She lives in Ohio with her family and writes in her spare time.

Download Free Books!
http://MendonCottageBooks.com

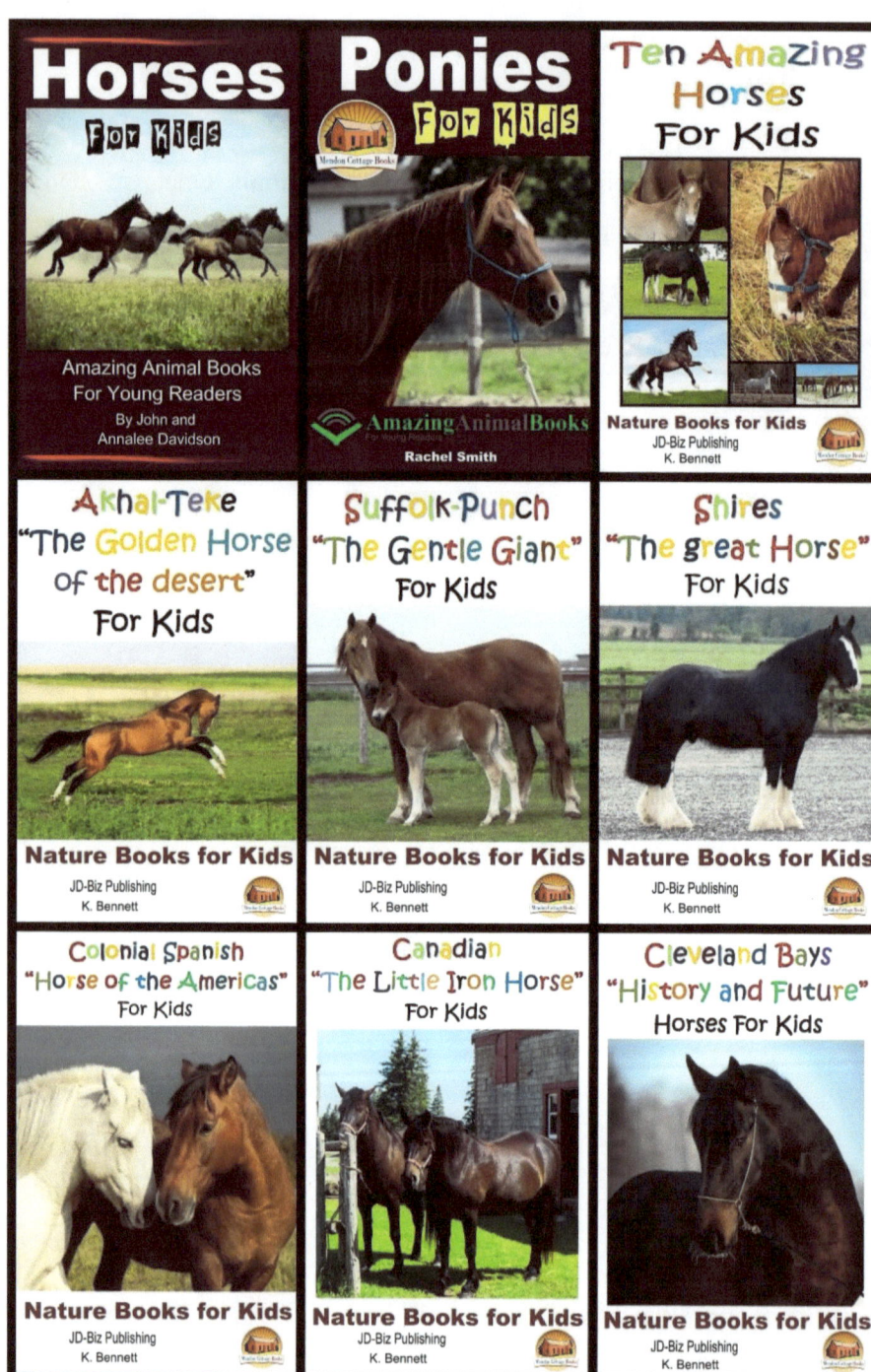

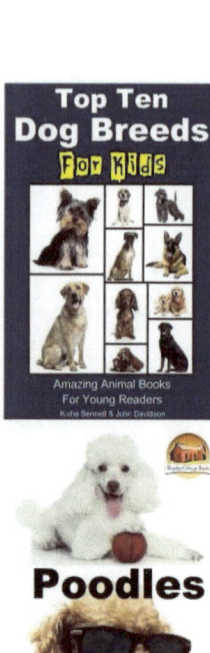

Top Ten Dog Breeds For Kids

Amazing Animal Books For Young Readers

Kisha Bennett & John Davidson

German Shepherds

Dog Books for Kids

K. Bennett

Bulldogs

Dog Books for Kids

K. Bennett

Dachshund

Dog Books for Kids

K. Bennett

Poodles

Dog Books for Kids

K. Bennett

Labrador Retrievers

Dog Books for Kids

K. Bennett

Rottweilers

Dog Books for Kids

K. Bennett

Boxers

Dog Books for Kids

K. Bennett

Golden Retrievers

Dog Books for Kids

K. Bennett

Puppies

Dog Books For Kids

Amazing Animal Books

By John Davidson

Beagles

Dog Books for Kids

K. Bennett

Yorkshire Terriers

Dog Books for Kids

K. Bennett

Dogs

Top Ten Dog Breeds For Kids

Amazing Animal Books For Young Readers

Zahra Jazeel & John Davidson

Cats For Kids

Amazing Animal Books For Young Readers

K. Bennett & John Davidson

Foxes For Kids

Amazing Animal Books For Young Readers

Zahra Jazeel & John Davidson

Wolves For Kids

Amazing Animal Books For Young Readers

By John Davidson and Virginia Fidler

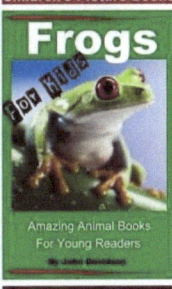

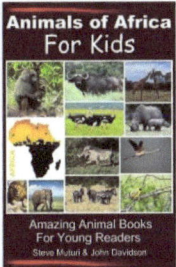

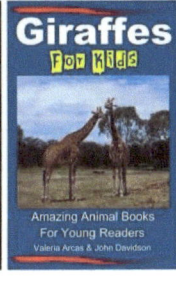

Our books are available at

1. Amazon.com

2. Barnes and Noble

3. Itunes

4. Kobo

5. Smashwords

6. Google Play Books

Download Free Books!
http://MendonCottageBooks.com

Publisher

JD-Biz Corp

P O Box 374

Mendon, Utah 84325

http://www.jd-biz.com/

www.ingramcontent.com/pod-product-compliance
Lightning Source LLC
Chambersburg PA
CBHW050912290526
45792CB00002B/793